# TAXONOMY OF THE MISSING

# TAXONOMY

## OF THE

# MISSING

[poems]

## Lisa Lewis

WINNER OF THE 2017 TENTH GATE PRIZE
Leslie McGrath, Series Editor

THE WORD WORKS
WASHINGTON, D.C.

*Taxonomy of the Missing*
Copyright © 2018 Lisa Lewis

Address inquiries to:
The Word Works
P.O. Box 42164
Washington, D.C. 20015
editor@wordworksbooks.org


Author photograph: Roger Mullins
Cover design: Susan Pearce


LCCN: 2018931392
ISBN: 978-1-944585-19-8

# Acknowledgments

Many thanks to the editors of the journals where the poems listed below first appeared, sometimes in slightly different form.

*American Literary Review*: "Taxonomy of the Missing"
*Art Focus Oklahoma*: "Quadriptych"
*Carolina Quarterly*: "The poems about clothing"; "Seasons Said"
*Cloudbank*: "Petition for a Plastic Procedure"
*Florida Review*: "Prove Me Wrong"
*Four Way Review*: "Jesus Devil Curse"
*Grist Online*: "Alibi"; "New Politics"; "Feminism"
*Guernica*: "She Gets to Him First"
*Hampden-Sydney Poetry Review*: "Privacy's the matter of light"
*Kestrel*: "Forms of Vice and Intemperance"
*Knockout*: "He Considers the Advantages of Staying Awake"
*New England Review*: "Dry Hollows"
*No Tokens*: "After the Hurricanes"; "Disobedient"
*Pembroke*: "Postbellum"
*Plume*: "Scoop Up Broken"
*Sugar House Review*: "Cure"
*Tampa Review*: "Class Warfare"
*The Meadow*: "Rig"
*Tusculum Review*: "Cormorant"
*Tusculum Review Online*: "A Slipping Between Seasons"
*Warning: Poems May Be Longer Than They Appear: An Anthology of Longish Poems*: "Cinema Verité"
*WomenArts Quarterly*: "Autodidact"
*Zócalo Public Square*: "The Last Place"; "Departure in the Key of Restraint Minor"

Thanks too to the Oklahoma State University
for the time and support to complete this volume,
and to Dinah Cox, who reads everything.

*in memory of Joyce Osburn James*

# Contents

It's only a branch like any other
green with the flare of life in it
and if I hold this end, you the other
that means it's broken

broken between us, broken despite us
broken and therefore dying
broken by force, broken by lying
green, with the flare of life in it

—Adrienne Rich
from "The Art of Translation"

# Alibi

It was one of those years when things were turning all the same.
One week the great fish bearing isotopes to shore, even the milk
       for infants aflame, their mouths black barnacles.
Another week soldiers dancing to a beacon of silence, everybody
       hurry up and die.
We were sneaking extra time at our screens. We wanted to budge
       but could not for so much chickenwire, so many ancient
       slabs of tin. The sexual writhings we watched as we
       pleased, cranking the vibrations so the ceiling fans
       above us rained.
Sometimes we did charity work. There might be a wig in it for
       somebody, a pink dutchboy. Somebody set up registration,
       all we had to do was form a line.
And if it was someone we had bowed to long ago now persecuted,
       we read the reports with sorrow. *Any ideas?* we said. *We*
       *need ideas, do you have one?*
The cautious among us forbade it, and the rest of us read the
       reports, signed or not. Something bashed holes in the
       barn doors and now anything could get in.
It was the cruel dictatorship of the rich or the cruel dictatorship
       of the foreigns. An old woman we had known when
       we were children, capable of sticking bones in her blind
       face, was being driven away. She was two times too
       much, like a cat lady. In the photographs she might've
       been even more.
How had she gotten by? We had helped her. If not for our hands
       and our backs—and often she swore at us to work
       harder, we had not forgotten—she would've fallen long
       ago so we would not be bothered now when we are
       close to stumbling ourselves.
She has been wrong all along, the reports say. She has claimed
       things that are not hers and she has said she is better
       than she could possibly be. Her face takes the planes of
       an animal's. Her face takes the animals' food, arranged
       in paper sacks, unopened.

We swallowed the peace of a glass of milk. We held our arms
        straight up like the wings of flies. We wanted to see her
        as she had been—was she a dissolving statue?—or we
        wanted to wait for the night to rise in shared rightness.
*We left her long ago because we knew,* we said. In the dusk of the
        hollow mountains, the sadness of the mountains that
        low through their horns like the shepherds that could
        not survive on those stones, she has toiled too long,
she should not have gone there alone and she never called us.
        We had to read the reports, and we are women.
How would we unfurl the net and draw it across our hidden
        waters, and what thin snails would be snared?
We are good at staring backwards down the road to the peak
        and declaring too many hairpin turns.
At death someone pays a fistful at a gate, but if the gate is
        broken, no one passes. Didn't she break the gate with
        her own hands?
Her right hand seized the lock and squeezed. Let her go on.
        Ask us to read the reports
with one eye, the pupil like a pool for drowning, and the words
        that float back up are the ones that say she is gone.

# Dry Hollows

We lived at the foot of a mountain.
As children we learned to count the toes.
Rough chunks of rock sticking
where they touched so we couldn't forget
how many. Always someone calling:
does it add up? Strong, sweet flavors
pushed out of palmate blossoms, a golden line
up the hillsides where later we followed
a yelping we thought must be foxes
but we never glimpsed the coats,
*devil of devils, ghost of ghosts*. Our hands closing
on edges and legs lifting bodies, step by step,
over sandstone, or coal, veins like sorrow
emptying, bodies on stretchers, their faces true
smut, search and misfortune.
We might've lit a smudge pot in remembrance.
Songs: yes, we sang, but at our loudest
we heard outside our own echo
something without melody. Who steals wood
to make fire? When we attained
the grove, a circle of oaks should've risen.
We wandered another kind of rut, a groove
dug for the sake of stealing, selling,
and stealing again, hiding machine tracks,
smoothing stingy turf over wounds.
We read a sign telling promises.
Words skipped here and there to make it true,
an easy pitch, our hands with fingers bent back,
no leather to cover them, where it said we had a gift.
We needed the mountain, the mouth carved
open to show the fangs, and we could trust them
not to bite. We could trust the hero
in his cap like a cookpot, dull boots, lowering himself
on a chain, or a vine, into darkness

for a story only he could tell and we must not ask
wrong questions. We were a generous people
then, tall, more like saplings than the flocks
of rhododendron that gathered to listen
as we talked. They rubbed their thick joints
like the legs of crickets, respectfully,
a tribe of believers not so much
on their knees as watchful and stern.
By then gravel roads bled when it rained.
We walked, we ran, we smelled urgency
resembling the stink of marigolds
rubbed between the palms to repel flies, wings
stuck together in the presence of gods.
We said. We sang. Then it was the sun
drifting like a feather into some kind of gorge.
Who painted those stripes? They're not water.
Someone said *a giant* and someone said *we've worked for this*
and someone lit a torch or cigarette
and where we stood rolled away as we stared,
quivering in its own wake like a sulfur cloud,
stirring the broody shell of guts unwound
from its caverns. Our shadows spread
flat before us, giving up. We walked
in a colorless steam that stained.
We had nowhere to go, no sack of moss, no biscuit.
It was a mountain, yes, exposed, breathing
its story of shame, hauled out
in crates and boxcars, turned into hard money
to pay for junk and buckets and a sun
rising late like a drunkard, lying
down in a nightgown of smoke.
Wallowing in the valley, the tiny flowers
of thyme, stars of memory and everything
we hadn't invented, photos we hadn't taken
on cameras we didn't own. We called ourselves artists.
We called ourselves tyrants. We followed a figure

drawn in charcoal, shaded with saliva. *Look,*
we said, *it's up ahead.* And we walked farther,
to climb the slope to a higher projection.
So many steep boulders and bounds,
staghorns, but as in the songs for dreaming
ourselves to sleep we only turned on our heels,
our reflections in muddy pools, we headed up
but spun irrevocably down.

# Cinema Verité

I. categorically not

what are you doing lying amongst pillows you said
it's not like you    the fairest one of all

we'd been watching Paul Newman movies
Paul Newman in *Hud* taking his shirt off

driving a Cadillac Paul Newman in *Sweet Bird of Youth*
driving a Cadillac taking his shirt off

you wanted a sleep mask  you dreamed I'd lift it
from your face    when you say *trick*

do you mean handstands or a deck of cards
when you say *dirt* would that be marl

scraped from the inner ear of the wheelbarrow
when you say *buttons* are you changing the channel

rummaging in the bedside drawer for a needle
lifting a sliver of thread to the lamplight

one more drop of magic potion
and we peel like postage stamps from slick paper

we'll be the people who tunnel under the river
solitary as moles    when somebody else picks up

the check we amble away arm in arm laughing
you couldn't see around the bowl of cut dahlias

we were triangulated on a grid like grilled cheese
the crusts removed   I was complaining again

losing my pen under the covers
drawing knee cartoons under there on the real thing

the night light's pony carousel galloping me awake
not you  you crimped your bow tie

for my next performance the prairie skirt
I refused to zip    scripts in the latin of kine

the last season crawling into place on a sled
shouting mush mush

ejecting the sloppy sibilants
like deodorant out of a can   a hawk from a wrist

a bent nail clawed from a board
when you say *clear* is it the package I didn't unwrap

when you say *shine* is it the pigeon's neck
the shoes hurrying back into the closet

the morning approaching with its long bars
to beat the house back into the shadows

II. movement de lune

shinnies up its own twig    fish twine
who has seen the paper plate marked little *a*

and the light emerging with its back turned
gray as a curlicue of dove feather the cat left behind

gray as the cat's listless paws
I thought you were done with people

you said    I thought you had slithered into the world
of machines    I came of age in that world

the lyrical blueprints clipped under leggy bulbs
appetite itself plugging a hole in its face

a cigar stub shedding miniatures of its leaves
the work trimmed to fit a green box

earthbound    four unknowns seated
around a card table planning their next heist

the scheme to introduce
themselves to the dying entrepreneur

everything adapted to that now like buttercups
the few petals the tall nodding weak stalks

cancel it    I cancelled it    didn't show up
I left them all standing around waiting

while the sky zipped its wet suit
another lazy white boy urged the horses on

III. misbegotten notions

I never sewed you said let alone stocked a sewing kit
I said I had a blue basket    wait it was ruddy of high

lightness    pinking shears to clack against the table top
raising the unconvincing profile of a partial body

from cotton woven in a casing like intestines
the goal was to get everyone to look this way

but did you mean burlap punishing the ankles
or the stars cartwheeling east

when you say *trick*
glasses do you mean eyeballs

dingly-dong on springs    when you say *glasses*
do you mean the spectacles of history

the founding of cities    civilizations
now only rumors    bronzes of nurses and nursing dogs

who has a mind for dates when you say
*mind* do you mean that jug we found on our walk

brimming something neither of us would sniff
as the moon shakes off its determination

we see it in daylight mottled as any bad apple
but now like the merest dot punched in

mechanically are there people licensed as carpenters
here    tipping their paint caps for other people

if they can find walls with windows    women sewed tents
for the military    nobody wanted to strafe that little

cloven foot of needle across her fingers aiming for seam
nobody wanted to be pierced through with a puncheon

middle c on the piano struck one knuckle
the major chords that hum nothing

open the lid    the wires you must not touch
bare-handed    your sweat will rust the notes

leave friction to the cotton glove
the technician's leather bag beside her on the bench

IV. division of labor

you hum to the clink of tumblers
exiting the dishwasher like cartoon fairies

meanwhile back in the garage I'm building new cats
from the hair in the corners    a satisfied tabby

licking umber paws    dust to dust
not everyone understands justice cracking in half

on the perforation    no chips no cut fingers
our shared bathroom stocked with bandages

at the strike of the clear moon we bleed in unison
not what you think    only where we suffer staring

we know what we're doing    we don't discuss
the knives desexed    the cabbages neither dangerous

nor erotic    throwbacks to an era when work fell together
with love and lay in the grass so long it bleached

pale beneath promises    when you say *crane*
do you mean fine arched bird or mechanical aptitude

when you say *neck*  do you mean isthmus of skull
and shoulder or the plain pastime of a slippery mouth

what are we going to do tonight   you say and I pretend
not to hear so you'll say it say it say again

I'm already riding my broom to the ceiling
where light's tender spider spins askew

a hammock for our breeze   safely away
from garden's shards    last century's night-

bloomers perfumed with the root of rage
buried from which they aim to shoot

once we dug them up   black carrots
these are for you   I said   wear them well

we have stones to chisel   stews to simmer
you chose the fattest amulet to cleave

the tendril end profusely sorry for its sins
the round one from which the flower burst

soft in your balancing hand as any sane person
would whisper from a distance

look those women are keeping a secret
now they are telling    what is that language

whatever we guess will be wrong

# Feminism

When it rained all spring, we stayed away
From the usual parties, even the weddings
And midnight showings of our favorite mysteries.
Maybe we already knew the solutions,
But we had held hands in the shadows anyway,
Chaste as fatherless young. By now I understood
Everything about the view from the window:
A bench rotting to lichen, the drops that swelled
Like blisters from the gutters, and the gush
That might mean sailing into another world,
As if I took up oars and shoved through
The swirling waters where the weight of song
Embellished a kind of throne. *Languid*, I said
And meant it. I wondered if my sisters
Missed my practice and collections, the clarity
I handed around like a candy dish, caramel
Tugging the molars and the teary spike
We blamed on sweetness and reluctant saving.
The measly yellow flowers of sedum and ground-
Blooming roses burst like apricots where I
Could not step. Belief tasted my mouth
And found it bitter. *Where are they dancing tonight?*
I asked my little dog and the silence he could not
Break seemed to me to prove my broken point.
When the others spoke of him their breath
Smelled of salt, or spite. Every day, still
Lightning split the limbs from the trunks,
And the bees slept off their poisons, but I
Understood more than the mere clay.
I stroked my dog's head until my hands
Smelled of his tangible sins. I had lavished
An ache on the female world, my contentious
Moment pitted against superior beauties,
And its failure washed through the moving clouds

Like runners who come in last and are simply
Relieved to slow down. This way weeks
Of weather stand for everything we can't control,
And no triumph shakes the gray from the sky
Without the price of passion, or paralysis,
That we must not win. The last night I released
The dog to race the yard, dry then, forceful
With orderly thorns, and my closest, oldest
Friend remarked—a pronouncement for all—
*He's like a show dog.* When our chorus of womanly
Murmurs rose to agree, I should've known:
I should've known. They waited a long time to leave
That night, as if they honestly couldn't move.
And who can bear that? Who can face it again,
Knowing what's lost, and that the rains will flush
The old joys away, or we can claim as much,
If in the ulterior we are made to meet again?

# Forms of Vice and Intemperance

*Not the shape of the space but that I stand here*
*knowing: the inch, the meter, the june bug*
*tumbling in grass where the wheelbarrow rolled.*

I had been driven back to my parents' house,
shamed back empty-hearted.
I had not been the woman a man wanted.

I had not been able to pay my phone bills,
who was I talking to? I remember
only the topic of conversation

and the humiliating tears, the futile hope
I would bring him down. I can't repeat
the accusations: I told him what he knew.

But I had also lost my mother's love.
She had wanted to be rid of me,
marrying off the unnamed daughter

to a family with a history, farm life,
song, the callous of intellect deep
as the skin of art and high finance.

From a previous century, it seemed,
me in green skirts and bodice of lace
torn by fingers, repaired by metaphor.

If only I had corseted my own breath.
My friend, though—she was worst.
I am waiting for her now,

in this space with the rock garden
she hates and the hosta bed she hates
and the dream she hates but will not say so:

it drove her mad. She locked me out
of her hospital room. She adored
and she lied, she became herself

that summer when dogs drank
from watermelons smashed in the road
and were themselves destroyed by wheels.

When will she come? When will she read
my letters and reply? She can't forgive
my lost suffering. She returns it

like a faded platter, a lottery ticket,
a fur coat no one would wear in this heat,
this era. We are going to die soon,

I want to say. I have paced out this plot,
I have summoned the animals home.
I have shaken the dirt from their beds.

These many weeks of rain raise a stink
from the honeysuckle and the lilies
of day, blue hyssop of night.

Where have you hidden now,
pill bottles and milk jugs and a hammer
to beat the nails peaceful? One night

I called him again, and he was cooking,
he said, pretending to be happy to hear
my wicked voice. He was just lifting

the pan from the stove. There was no time
to talk, he had begun his race to win, but I had
time, and I took my time, and I took up

standing, and walking, and standing,
and pacing, and standing and shouting
and screaming and keeping still.

I learned to live off bread and jam.
I fought my miniature wars. Here are
my relics. My own bare skull.

My terrible patience, worn to a point
with a spare shadow, and a bird flies over
this octagon, holding itself above.

# After the Hurricanes

September: weather for swimsuits—
my first adult one-piece,

black and white chessboard blocks.
I'm bending from the waist

into my own inverted initial,
sand dollar for the camera,

oil rig carving the horizon. Home
I'd twist the soles of my feet

to describe Rorshach tar spots—
*Bat. Washer Woman.*

*Malevolent Panda, Blinded.*
Wouldn't scrub off. Wore thin.

Long ago for a kid like me,
the Holiday Inn where runaways

Suzie and I holed up on stolen
credit cards. The night of strip

search, cops fired at our fleeing car—
shooting blanks, a good bang,

what I'd been up to in darkness
after the bar where men would've traded

us for rope. Too soon to guess what
would become of mussels, skates, rays—

double names for what moves us,
flexed to budge weight or skidding

feet and ankles scuttling a cloud's
polish the afternoon the worst

comes true: tsunami fisting a nuclear plant,
chain of thick money, earth's blood libel,

CEOs buying up the last cool spots.
Now when I walk into waves,

legs compassing, the acid burns
only weak things, gone anyway.

The wind wings pebbles on a plate
and the grains swirl like oats

under my heels. This is a short life
we're having, Atlantic.

Those who knew you before, Gulf, see
you've lost your looks. Those coins

on the beach are not dollars.
I don't believe they came from shells,

limned skin, stink of pelican fish.
Ghost crabs sidle beneath black beads.

Wherever they're aiming,
they don't look here.

# New Politics

It's all cochineal lipstick and sunglasses
in the notebook now, as if nothing happened
but a slow dance everyone watched from the pits
of envy by the gym doors. That's what you say

when you show up late to your last chance,
a slender pencil in the way of hope dangling
from your throat on a chain, keeping up
appearances or holding close every slow second

before you're not surprised the all-expenses-paid trip
sails without you. Sometimes you find your name
carved in soapstone, floating in oil. You measure
reincarnations in iris petals or quills on a cat's tongue.

You spruce vases of error and dare Loves Me Not.
You accept a job in a pharmacy, but the mortar
and pestle carry tales and the ampules snap
their purses shut, convinced of thieving

intentions, though when they wish to sleep
side by side, you bed them in cotton and close
the box tight for the darkness they deserve.
You sign up for harp lessons. You coif your hair

to match. When your fingers renounce the lesser notes
they rise to meet your breath, but you refuse the song
and the ghost of song for the sake of strange treason,
the past, or merely pity. *Come again*, you're whispering

like a woman seeing off the minister and thinking, *please,*
*not soon.* As if you could ballast this body
so long it pitched into an open door, and the key
warming your hand to lock it in case

pursuit closed in and you needed to run hard.

# A Slipping Between Seasons

Bowl or wicker basket—
sense might empty, or stay,

mine. Pecans, matchbooks,
the stuff of casual capture,

canopy or steakhouse,
cigarette machines, doorknob

stalks dumping stale packs
to stick and coins, always

the last, chattering blind
into a tin cup. Tell me

I should've known. I'd erase
the long backstory,

fingertip riding the lines.
My best trick's disappearance,

someone said, so I changed
the names: thorn to thimble:

stockingcap, mime.
Nighthours I force my arms

like stems by my stitched sides,
and smoke interrupts the clouds,

coverup, none too elaborate
for what psychologists call the will

to be caught. Well, I tried that,
rifling trashbins for simulacrum,

or pills. Then, vividly, the sky
one second past gray noon,

a stunt flyer loop-de-looping,
the pasture nobody swore by;

and the yearling colts
traipsing my straight line

slow: fill me like that, upside-
downsy coffee cup, shimmering

pears, still life worth living,
despite debris, and listening

to whispers that strike up
loud and fade till what remains

is ringing, force of thickened
blood and disappointment,

matched twins: the sky's cold
comfort answers west, bright

before late colors I can't predict
but might guess, an old story,

good idea. All right, I'm staying.
I'm staying here. And facing

into the spaces I haven't filled.
Dense as stain between thin walls,

or the snapped twigs I can't reach
breaking the shape of the Indian

dogwood, I make my claim
like a star that only seems to fall

if you believe the earth, smudged
as a banjo, is all there is.

# Prove Me Wrong

The car I still drive has the old-fashioned windows you crank up
    and down.
Everyone I don't know that well forgets to lock it when they
    get out.
When I was seventeen and running with the boys who ran dope
somebody who didn't know me that well stuck his head in
the car window where I lay across the back seat with one
Steve somebody wriggling his skinny wrist
down the tight waistband of my ragged hem jeans
and hoping the other guy would see just as much asa I hoped
    he wouldn't
and who knows which strung-out teenager got a wish.
If I did I didn't get much, a bad rep and a gladness
shining like a quarter on pavement I wasn't obedient,
no churchgoer, no cheerleader, and when did that boy—
another one, not Steve, no bad girl's life has one bad boy in it—
tell me he was worried I was doing too much dope?
Skinny, unwashed, badass, hardass, I would've loved
to read the future, except nowadays there's nothing
but the music and the Oklahoma night pulsing
over the prairies like the last mothership cloud
to hover above the county of Payne and decide, leisurely, to
    move on,
we're a little too deep in the valley, and we look it.
Maybe for a day I imagined myself marrying
my rock star wannabe, his crunch of black curls, long
tapered pinky nail for dipping cocaine, he said, but all we did
was valium and fucking on a cold skin waterbed and praising
for lack of anything to say. Comparatively speaking,
we were it, and don't think I was unlacing boots
because we were already barefoot and don't think I liked
pleasing him or anybody but I pretended otherwise
and if I had a certain kind of smarts

I still would, but my name was fight, rage and spin and hide
from the spyglass of parents and good
girls and pretty girls except I looked fine
naked in the mirror that night drunk with Bill or whatever
his name was, and so did he, eyes gleaming like stop signs
but we didn't stop until he cuffed my ears, and somehow
the next day I turned into somebody with a secret.
I rode it bareback like a bull, I sounded like I was telling
the truth, the charade of crepe paper and parasols lingering
at the end of the darkness became my specialty and who didn't
        I fool?
The tricksters spinning red and black like poker chips
but they lost the bet, who's still alive? Who's cursing and spitting?
You're listening to her, and underneath all the claims
of needing a sweet story, sweet thing, bedtime drip drip drip,
you'll forget exactly the same moment you forget
all your promises you believed in and their objects—their fools—
taking good care, filing your paperwork in the metal case, too.

# Disobedient

Two women loved one another
　　　but would not say so
except to one another. After all,
　　　it was Oklahoma,
where forgiveness perched
　　　like a hawk on the power lines
stringing little hollow churches
　　　to one chain-gang necklace
sagging across the scalded plains.
　　　Those wings opened
only to sear down above arched claws
　　　to the backs of rabbits
and field mice. The Lord's angry
　　　huntress scorned the soft
bodies of all her unsuspecting prey,
　　　short lives quivering
to pieces, talon-torn. And women
　　　in love loved the flex
of potato peel and the crease
　　　of watercress
they coaxed from watered
　　　clay, sunburn and shade.
The early sprouts always curled
　　　to animal shapes,
they said, and they bought a dog
　　　to follow and watch
and dig between the rows.
　　　The worst that happened
was sometimes the strobe
　　　of helicopters overhead,
but they were used to it,
　　　their fathers military men.
Or the man next door yelling
　　　mistaken names

when the one who'd played high school
          softball mowed the lawn
in her undershirt. *Hey boy*
          *gimme dat gimme summa dat!*
Whatever that meant. It wasn't bad,
          she said. She said she thought
he meant she didn't have much.
          At night he might sneak out
to watch their windows,
          mouth ajar like a moon.
He'd like to say, perhaps, if only
          to himself, he'd snatched
a glimpse of that flat chest,
          to prove it wasn't just for girls,
the one girl, the taller one, at that.
          Or what if he caught them going
at it? He'd climb the cedar by the chimney,
          not to see but to hear or feel
sound jump of heartbeat—
          not like what he paid for
behind the warning screen
          *you must be 18 to enter,*
not the shuddering machine of breasts,
          taffy-pink stretched mouths
and manicures shoved everywhere,
          barbed as mannerly girl-tongues
should never risk with husbands,
          fathers, brothers, neighbors—
never any man. She guessed
          all that, and said she figured
she guessed right:
          men love law, she said,
and protocol, none of this *Fuck off*
          and *Get your hands out*
or coming up with answers.
          She could turn back

to her work with words or love
        or tossing a tennis ball
hard and high for the setter mix
        to fetch, and if her body
said its piece in language
        a man next door
translated into rage or scorn,
        he never wore a shirt at all,
she said, and he's got boobs.
        Big ones!
Overhead the sun winked back
        its own crude joke
as if to prove whose side it took.
        No clouds, no whispers,
no man's land or word or boot
        stamped down on concrete
heavy with its own idea, itself,
        weighed down dirty,
serious. The trees and mulch
        and foxglove beds of woman's
land cooled open secrets,
        eyeshot, earshot.

# Privacy's the Matter of Light

You're dealing cards around the table,
>        the hands you've won criss-crossed
and a highball sweating a coaster
>        out of reach, counter's precipice.
Later you'll dice beef for chili
>        and rinse snow peas for salad,
but it's early, just past sunset,
>        and the blinds aren't drawn
this hour for strolling. The last children
>        on bicycles tune out
their parents' calls,
>        and the woman who walks
whippets, one blond, one tawny pinto,
>        ignores the cop who on weekends
knots a bandana around his head
>        and straddles a Harley's
nostalgic thunder.
>        This is the hour of glimpsing
what we missed, or guessed,
>        decided against or never dreamed,
when to be inside the frame
>        of plate glass is to be the star
aligned with stars next door,
>        each innocuous plot unfit
for drama unto itself but worth
>        peering into one step at a time
outdoors. This is the hour to trade
>        spectacle for secrecy, stealing
to horizon's scalloped hem
>        where the sun's wake lingers,
now plush velvet you can't see
>        from beneath the ceiling fan
where friends receive the blessing

of treys and aces
and you tell jokes and do not confess
    what the street can make
of your immodesty: games
    that gather in sight,
the rectangle strobed by night
    and slowly whirling blades,
you pushing back
    your ladder-backed chair,
time to start dinner,
    another round first, gin?
And your arm rising arcsome
    as the clock signals angles,
your shadow receding
    through the curtain's graph.
This is the end of witnessed
    joy of evening. Morning,
now on no one's mind,
    begins reversal, when passersby
glancing houseward face darkness
    from which the view's expanse
zooms in grassblades, dry
    violets' coiling mousetails,
rough-shed river birch,
    sedans' lush scalding hoods,
one arch backdrop
    of blue sky south and west
to north and east, everyone
    minding new business.

# Class Warfare

My kind oils its native tongue
        megaphone-style.
I speechify, and the sentence spins
        on its thin dime, spent
calling back my brethren led away.
        Now I'm pumping a jack handle.
Now I aim the flashlight
        down my throat
and read the membrane's graffiti.
        I utter my own name
and a streak of bees
        erupts and stings my last
nerve's yards. Where'd everybody
        go? I dish up a concatenation,
oranges, fingernail moons, and god.
        The wafer tastes
like saliva, or the original
        disintegrating power tools,
miniaturized children
        like a bad debt. You can quote
me on that. Eventually I get around
        to dropping hot verbs in broth
where they brew a tea like the herbs
        a woman chews to abort.
That's as honest as it comes
        around these parts, this hair
taking bows on the white line.

# Postbellum

If anyone asked why you have to find that house
you would not be generous replying,
driving this neighborhood days now, slowing
at each driveway, checking maps, old and new,
creased glovebox copy and cellphone
treble mispronouncing the graphed world.
Your mother's ambition—to move
to this street, sidewalk curving like a stream
at the base of the hill, which she would watch
from an upstairs room, empty most hours,
most days—came true, whatever peace
there was in staircase and clematis fertilized
in pots on a deck both sunny and shaded.
White woman in the northerly south:
she was no expert, but she tried,
and the plum cake sagged with rum
in its frivolous pan, the silk blouses
murmured their names from a dustless
closet, and the antique wicker survived
repair as long as no one sat down.
And the husband who must not be disturbed—
the most valuable feature of the architecture,
who came out only after five, for ice and water
and the transparent grain that passed for water
in a short glass. He knew his part
best. That's where the trouble came in,
and for all they know it's still running
like the most successful musical
they never heard of. If only no one
had discovered how little they'd seen
above that horizon of shaggy bark
and leaded windows that weren't.
A shame to steal from the elderly—

furniture, cornmeal in a box.
You could tell them it's over now,
no more worries about making
people believe, if you could just remember
the address, but what remains is false:
you're walking home from a secret park
where you lay on a secret picnic table
and feared for your safety as you'd been trained,
but nothing happened and though you rushed
home to tell danger's truth, you stopped
to clear someone's garden,
and when she caught you,
she said *keep what you've stolen*—
moppy fistful, daylilies and shrub rose.
That was the story you told in the kitchen,
years before you were found out
as worse, much worse, than childhood predicted,
and maybe they learned too much, maybe
their own failures: go ahead, blame yourself
for the grace you thought you saw through
at the same time you held it above
the hungry faces of your parents,
fools for a prize they could not win,
and while you're at it, the story of the south
and its various white flags, handprints
sewn in starry yarn. All of it.
Not just a week driving streets
changed since you walked them but what's left
of eternity, returning to the dead
as if they waited, or wanted to, knowing
what everyone knows today about their dreams
and your voyage back to accuse.

# Seasons Said

I bore away the old boards, boat battery, garter snake
beheaded by shovel. I bled rust for the chain link fence.
I suited up to strip poison ivy, pigweed, amaranth tall

and broad as an ordinary man, sameness of crabgrass
splashes like summer sparklers, widening, bleaching
twine-tight roots. I loaded my wheelbarrow

with the anguished skull of the lost cat no one spayed
and the stop sign bereaved of its ice cream truck, still
whistling pipes under the breath of Capricornus.

I took the screwdriver's one buck tooth to a barrel of oil
worth nothing but the iron filings of the lean old motors
it greased. I rolled it away, spilling a panful to stain

the asphalt no one on my street would forgive.
I double-bagged the trash, the trouble, luckless growth
of native flora uncultivated for beauty because their sisal

clasping the throats of the blessed clematis kills.
I steamed the gristle of hate away. I dug it up. I severed
worms, hell surrendered its dew below their naked reach.

The bare earth's readiness declared *bring me roots,*
in clay, in moistened hands—a poplar tree, dwarfed,
in a bucket. Sage, cress, bristling bluets, thyme

in vulgar flavors. I planted taxonomies I knew not
and named them for saints and ponies. I pried
a place for a clump of mallow striped like a jungle hybrid

and it smothered itself in shadow. Everything beneath
knelt down. I offered the spilt remainders of my kitchen's toil,
jigsaw morsels it couldn't swallow, and it swore obeisance

to the spirit of loam. A chorus hummed from grains
and grass. And it all came back, the tangle, the mass,
the weight of my labors like a jacket hooked on a fence:

the days dripped sweat, and the earth hurried to save itself,
shade from sugar, millet, eyespot, honeybees' soft spines.
Whatever I'd done it changed. *This is no office*

*for cubicles*, it might've said or sung, but I had found
some kind of room for rakes and spades and a water hose
I coiled snake-shape behind my house. No killing left

in any of us, not much—just to keep a clearing,
beds for the comings and goings of a few spare blooms
I preferred, the rest whatever the clay would hold.

# Cure

A rock crashes a window, sole
intention of the boy who threw it
echoing by the skull of a pigeon

pecking grain. The bird's
gross pitcher of airy bone,
lifting, whistles like fingers to teeth.

I never learned the trick.
My face grew towards the sun,
under glass. But my friend

says he's dying. Each conversation
he's drawn the line closer. Five years, two,
he's tearing a gauze of sky, and if

we described the effort between us
he'd meet my eyes, formal,
quick in the way of shame.

Once my gaze dusted sand
leaking back to sea. I heard talk, glanced
sideways. Singer on a hill, spotted

heifer stretching neck to browse
leaves across pipe fence,
lizard sunning spotted spine—

I waited to know before I spoke.
I waited not to be wrong.
A man whose stiff back

I whispered behind surprised me,
bending to pick a thorned rose,
scooping it to his chest: no, it was

a cat. Grotesque legs like a woman's
curved thumbs, obese in limp chinchilla,
voice on tongue like a slice of cheese.

*I love her*, he said. *I hope she lives
forever*. I was sure he'd done it:
say and it shall be. Simple blessing

for a tabby: eternal life. Now I know
to say it to whomever's due to fail,
and hope's a rope to tug a body free.

It's a symptom like signals
flashing stop, taillights shorted
in the shirttail night on a mud road,

rodeo, nip and tuck, hammered nail.
I hope we live forever. I hope
you do, and may it be no worse

than you're used to:
the usual, not the beautiful, slow
as a broken back, healing

without hands laid on.
My hope's a fact. My hope's a rowboat
shearing a path in lake's chill

center where the graph reflects
star, planet, all the same
from cure's distance, vein that bursts

from the brain, stumbling beat-up
saddle horn, hatstain, to the absolute,
unconfounded, ordinary heart.

# Jesus Devil Curse

If there's one thing nobody wants,
      it's a mare lame in both fronts.
You pinch the fetlock
      arteries for the digital pulse.
You pack the shod hooves
      with turpentine and sugar
to draw the soreness.
      You thumb the jugular for a dose
of horse tranquilizer. You run
      water for mud to cool her.
You pull the shoes with pliers,
      because somebody made a mistake
nailing shoes, a big-
      shouldered man, mouthy,
full of Jesus and guitar
      songs and a daughter with a bad
heart and marching orders.
      Listen, he talks while he's working,
looks like he got a little carried
      away. Now here's a lesson.
Here's a basket of lessons,
      a burning cedar tree of lessons,
horsehide to hammer to a tree
      of lessons you memorize.

The bony column ends in the so-
      called coffin. Hoof-shaped,
it balances a whole horse.
      Don't let sand and clay
come close. Any fool knows
      that half-inch spares the kingdom.
Jesus won't tell his secret,
      coffin bones like a compass south.

Coffin bones a water witch down.
           Jesus boy coaxed her close to hell.
Jesus boy hammered the door
           of horn and carved initials.
I'm looking for a hole
           to bury a horse. She's watching
the empty pasture:
           cedars like scarecrows
where their crowns died branching.
           Iron posts, ghost fence.
Hawks slide the sky
           like knives slicing fat meat,
a rubbery parting of clouds.
           A pond spreads flat
as wax paper downwind,
           smudge of water shine.
Someone says, the pond's low,
           we need rain. Someone says,
that would be a pretty pasture
           if we mowed. Those trees
break the blades. I never learned
           how to fix the broken blades.

She doesn't lie down but she
           can't walk. She's watching
the empty pasture.
           She doesn't want to miss
crow or frog or spun web
           or cross stuck with nails
for shoeing horses. All day,
           hobbles to the water barrel.
Drinks like someone deserted,
           dying. One day
a man drove the gravel
           on a mission. He hammered

and talked about television
        and Jesus and the whole story,
and if I keep telling this
        everybody's going to live
forever, including the ones
        who don't deserve it, not
because they floated to heaven,
        black wings trimming the fat
of the sky to quick, only
        because you caught me
rubbing something hard
        between my palms, not
a bit for a bridle, not
        a stirrup to rest my boot,
not a shovel to dig
        the grave, keeping my promise,
but she's just a horse
        so she can't be thinking
where will she go
        before she falls, and she looks
like I do when what happens
        to a man with a mouth and tools
for killing and a hawk
        shearing the sky and a devil
slapping its tail
        on hell's open door.

# He Considers the Advantages of Staying Awake

The ceiling fan stirs its pot and the night light
My wife insisted on waits for its chess partner
To settle into the rocking chair's creak.
The trick is to listen to no one's breathing,
The dog's noisy tracking, squirrels or strangers.
Once he woke himself wagging his tail
And sounded a worried alarm for the front door.
I don't know who to protect either.
What I learned doesn't work. Hunting elk,
Colorado winters, packing mules up
The high plains until we smear their hooves
With butter to force out the laming snow,
I didn't think what the hell can I do to cool
The summers? I count them backwards.
No set of tracks that doesn't return—
The creeks so dry they couldn't speak,
Cracked lips stuck on the first word.
I wanted music. I've lived here a long life
And never tuned a note or a string.
There lean the cottonwoods; post oaks;
Blackjacks: that's the high whine harping
Home, the wind, when nobody knew what
To do with the wood and nobody knows now.
That's what I hear, which ear I turn to
The pillow and which to sky, and the rings
Chasing the moon tonight rattle the hard way
Down. The San Bois mountains thick
With cedar, the mare's leg I rubbed
Tonight thick with blood and the water
The body pours on to heal. When the ice
Slipped its sheet my mule spun shoulder-
First and struck me so I thought I was alone
In eight layers of long johns and hard canvas.

I coughed all night in the tent where the stove
Pushed out its choke like a cow in labor,
And nobody, not me, not my friends old
And sleepless as I am, knew what to call the fog
But the wind calling after us at last. We waited
A while longer, though, spiraling down
The trail, my legs pronging both sides
Of that mule's slab back and nobody talked
Me into trying to climb off. It was the end,
Or would've been, not worth mentioning,
Like this bed I'm weighing with the light
My eyes draw down from blind bulbs
And my unplugged heart not stopping
And the dog and the woman who hates
Her work more than she hates me and the kids
Who moved out later than anybody wanted,
All buried in the shadows of their old rooms,
Their furniture shuffling its scuffed clogs,
And the prize I promise to bring home
But I never pick the right shapes off the shelves
Wherever I am, and except for the cold ride
I don't travel and when I do I burn diesel.
I'm not unhappy about it. It's winter, then
It's early for the fields to green, and when
I can't bend my back to tie my boots or set
A match to the trashpile, I'll stand up straight
And hike to the darkness down the road
And breathe deep all the way to the limestone.

# Rig

And now it pours its shadow over once-pasture, former-
Green-field, never-to-be-again-splay of ragweed and bermuda.

Rattlebox, sunflower, buckwheat-brown August to April,
The golden season—the nearly dead return so late

In spring the threat takes shape in dreams. *The end.*
That's the fear, isn't it? The earth won't bother

To try again? And now this, yellow as a construction site
pencil, stalk-straight, tall, poison tree of geology,

Red dirt bare as a rag everywhere around—
A couple trucks, a port-a-potty, and a man

In a denim jacket, back to the highway where I slow down—
But you can't stop and interrogate the guy,

Who may not even think it's a good idea—
He's not paid to get ideas—

To tear up the countryside in someone's back yard—
And yes, there's a neighborhood, poor Okie plains

Houses I've longed for through the seasons, venal
Decorations, bales of hay no animal would devour.

They might've owned this corner once but no more,
Small now in handmade pretension to the manmade

The rig stands for, in phallic detachment—
*There's that thing, that rocket—*

Not the lone workman's fault, to be born here,
To wish, himself, for whatever expands in a man

Beneath that spire. And I've been away,
Not long—it went up fast—

In weeks—but no one is here to make the case
For blood of bird or spume of thin, thin air.

No one is holding a protest sign. Nothing has spilled.
This is red dirt, not black, and there is no odor,

And no green, yet, not the kind you can't smell
Because it's numbers on paper and no longer the kind

I learned to recognize as winter rye, wettish blades
Laid down glossy as paint, cattle

Embarrassed at a distance, nibbling bark,
And the bark furrowed, flinging itself away.


•


What if you drove that road each day for years,
The ones you later recognized as superior,

And then appeared this monster of economy,
Of which we partake so we may be held accountable,

Punished if we kneel to suffer?
How would you sing of its stretch

Above your head, beyond muscle or flexion?
How bend the direction of its needle?

We are called to bleed together, thrust up your arm.
Let us stand side by side, dead brothers of poetry,

Neglected sisters, and find our tongues stitched
Into our cracked jaws, and pose for a group photo—

This is how we looked the year we remembered,
And next we glimpsed our faces

Reflected from dry ponds. We forgot
The mouthful names we'd loved to compass

On creased maps, and we sidled
The way we approach deaf gods.

Do we arrange notes on the clef of vines?
Manufacture this burned-out hymn,

Choir as wooden as the no-more
Trees, hands crossed on chests like the good-

Looking dead who had the sense to get it over with?
Lick your finger so the page sticks

To the grooves. We wait to fuel our travels
Into an emptier world on tires

That slick up dust and rocks. The far-off
Bristle of horizon nods, deep in the sleep

Of gravel before it's tested with bore
And the great tanks roll on their sides

Like everything that grazes, for the taste
Of what went down and then returned.

# Selling the Mineral Rights

We throw our jackets down and spread them
like picnic blankets, their linings visible,
bright satin or flannel plaid. We have walked here
to study and bow our heads. The grass crackles
like flame but there is no smoke. Something rises.
Something casts a shadow, something warns.
A woman is reading from a sheet of paper.
We catch the scent of the hungry who ate
before us. The meal includes meat and bread,
one mean smear of butter. The butter
blackens the bread, we eat it anyway.
The bread blackens our teeth, we give up
smiling. We turn our faces away, ashamed
of the organs inside our bodies, now also dark
and soft as if spoiled by frost. We're so close
to the base of the yellow blade shaving a little
off the heavens, cutting bare, we don't look up.
We slept before we began our walk. We opened
envelopes from the day's mail, we signed
the backs of checks, we learned new names.
Now that we're here even the shadows are yellow.
The whites of our eyes in the corners near
the snippet of watery pink can't conceal
what we've been drinking. We drink so much
our mouths don't hold the slosh. The stains
on our shirts spread. Dirty dirty. Drink drink.
Swallow the shadow whole. There's no grass
here anymore, only naked naked. Beetles,
striped hard, backwards, scrambling.
We take out our notebooks to study.
The noise begins, a dispassionate whirring.
In the circle of sound, we sit akimbo, knees
not touching, nothing touching, tongues that lie
in grooves like water fills gutters and runs

down, floods, fills oceans. We uncap pens
and fill them with something dark,
but it makes no mark upon paper or skin.
It smells but dark stain won't show.
The shadow drapes our heads
to hide the unholy hair, its bedeviled beauties.
Praise be to the god who destroys the names
and drinks the stain. Who let him in?
Who opened the gate to the passageway?
We opened the envelopes, we unfolded
the paper, we read numbers in sequence.
We had heard of this magic. We counted
until we could count no higher, and the rain
that dampened our shoulders sang
as we shivered, notes out of order.
*You will die by your own hand, you will*
*not know, you will die lying down*
*on the bare, on the bare, you will be naked,*
*you already are, you will die in the wallow*
*of magnetic arrows, cold and steel*
*and shadow from the rig your master*
and we rose to escape but the prayer
wrapped us up and the god pointed up
and we looked where he directed and the long
road darkened with the oil of days when
everything living lies down in the shadow
and the spire is yellow and the oil is yellow,
no, the oil is red with something to say
and the oil is brown with the story of earth
and the oil is not water because nothing
can swim and it is not air because nothing
breathes. It only burns with the promise
of burning, and the thrumming shudders,
throbbing, hollow bones to sand.

# The Last Place

*Let me be first to beg forgiveness.*
I draw back the curtain, past dusk.
They are gathering to throw pebbles
and paper cups, and their laughter
seizes the window frame and shakes.
Give me a moment to collect myself.
Let me be first to open the door
as I once tugged my skirt's unstitched
hem to cover my kneecap's domino.
Understand these seekers need
their place: mark life, water, breath,
clean grain, and bodies rushing together.
Stand not where they might stumble,
slow not their haste, and struggle not
to pin loose limbs to fleshless ribs.
They sing until the trees wriggle
into ropes, into worms. They cry out,
*We have so much farther to go!*
They count the toes inside their shoes,
miles scuffed, and I still shrink
behind my gate, I drop the handle
so it scrapes like a glove twisting
a jar lid, the brine spills. I measure
my love for what waits by the road,
an antler shed, a corpse's hard fur,
and the young travelers hurrying
to grow larger, to take up the city's work
before the moon corrects its zenith.
I learn my lesson aloud, I repeat it
like the failed closure of a mystery
or a dress. If I fell and they could not stop,
there would be no explaining—no time
for the first complaint—that I wanted
to rise on the gust of known smells,

the running, the racing to level
ground where the pace can speed up,
the secrets be revealed.

# Taxonomy of the Missing

You couldn't help feeling sorry for them.
They swaggered when they walked
And wept when they sat down.
The bones shone through their skin
Like long fluorescent tubes
Buzzing faintly with overuse.
They couldn't begin to live
Until the plane took off.
They couldn't check their phones
Until they could ping a closer tower.
The squirrels approached in the park
And they shrank, was this rabies?
The sere leaves of winter twirled
Like the young girls of May,
Fingertips touching, the circle
Spinning, but they felt no joy,
No lust to join in.
The boards clutching their houses
Together drooped top down
Like stockings sans garters,
Bluer, bluest. I had thought myself
The saddest of average humans,
But they were sadder and superior
And insisted by winking
Or jutting their bruised jaws
On not speaking of it.
I longed to commiserate—what
About the flat tires? What about
The gutters choking in their sleep?—
But they flew on wings
Like owls' wings, carrying less
Than they might've, and silent.
I told a story about deer
And they listened for the tock

Of cloven hooves on brick,
Refusing to believe them visible.
*Do you know I'm here?*
One of them asked and retreated
Before I could think of an answer.
I didn't want to hurt anybody.
I outlined a shadow like a corpse.
I wished I'd changed the subject
To the price of my script signature.
I was opening a jar of mustard
For my supper. I moved
Across the earth searching.
Before long, I could tell
I was still alone,
At least insofar as my own kind,
My close kin, tolerated
Only a little light on their faces,
And I preferred to glance down.

# The poems about clothing

are not warm enough for winter.
Though we shiver and tug their seams,
their buttons slip the loops.
Rub them like silk between thumb
and fingers. They spark with static,
but you may not plug them in.
Your daughter may light a match
to the mattress, killing your little dogs,
but the poems about sweaters
and ties that wiggle in wind—
goodbye, tree branch,
farewell, strangled trachea—
will spare your life only afternoons
when the sun's flares burn like paraffin
and songbirds gather string.
Expect the fur to grow thick on deer
now rumored in poems to be rutting:
lucky the hooved who wear neither
sleeves nor cuffs nor brassieres.
We measure our tunics' lingering tails.
We tag the feet, we sell. The dresser
is stuffed on patches and rags.
The poems about belts and elastic
hold nothing up or together.
We sharpen the shears
with the carnation blades
and chew the fabric to petals.
Fetch the broom, this floor's heaped
for sweeping, threads that weave
like centipedes, pills to swallow
of rayon. The plan was always to undress
dress. We assumed a natural order.
Poems twirled like skirts embroidered
with spaniels, poems so snug

at the collar the fleshy jowls
ripened like plums. On the clothesline
or the bookcase, a flapping.
Wings as of vellum, eyelids lined
in ink's iron gall, or the swaddling
that pinned our ankles
before our first glottal burrs.

# She Gets to Him First

She's pretending not to wipe away the cobwebs'
        ceiling geometries, the gnats
fussing the children's eyes.
        The room's twin corners lock down.

She's been standing here all afternoon,
        waving her broom like a torch.
She can't hear the crack of tires on gravel,
        revival of the sun's absent-minded scorch

trumping November as it orbits July,
        a pencil eking out a list of things not to do:
the first errand this week neglected
        last week. *The trouble with night*

*is morning*, she's singing, wringing out socks
        over a tub, grinding salt into the bloody spots.
When her head aches, she can't taste
        the boxed macaroni. When she weeps,

she rubs the lamp's sinuses and they burst
        like a pumpkin coughing up seeds. Simultaneity:
a descriptive term, when she crashes the obligatory
        walk and the wall framing

the highway crumbles, but already a figure
        neat as a staple gun tumbles ahead, the social downfall
of her sister who whispered a name and didn't stop
        running until the matching face shone

on a refrigerator door like a recipe for a sandwich
        or an old joke about an idol. *I have to get over this.*
She's speaking in rhythm again,
        whining like her oldest son.

It won't be the last time he filches money
        from her beaded purse. He's got a voice
like a bellows, a closet muddy with shoes.
        She's taken care of him since she pressed him like a leaf.

He sticks like melted rubber to his own hands.
        She learns pity that day, and the next,
and the next, and then he confesses, and then
        she bows to applause.

# Autodidact

*Sworn off,* I said, waving away invitations
To all the trouble I once loved, like sweeping floors
For the sake of dance or scrubbing sinks
So later sons could take their brunch
Without reminders of last night's crusted
Disappointments, cheese-fried or otherwise.
I who had coaxed stains from linen with sweet
Soda and stammered out secret alphabets
Over the high chairs of small lords had stepped off
Shift to stay there, and the longer I recoiled
From broom-tufts and the winking eyes of needles
Honed on the rage of nighttime lamps, the later
I stayed up reading diaries I stole from my own shelves.
Whoever whispered on the stairs tiptoed
Elsewhere eventually. Every time I'd tried this before
I aimed my pointy peep-toes direct to gravel's
Jaded heart and returned wearing the uncut
Tresses of the shamed and lonely. Now,
Though I still could not make out the words
On certain pages I held to unshaded light,
I believed I would learn them once and for all
If I had to write them myself. The stars counted
Clouds under their breath, waiting,
The windowpanes ticked with thwarted moths,
And the shapely letters dropped down
From on high, each spiral in its own sound,
Where I caught them on my tongue like snow.

# Departure in the Key of Restraint Minor

The car was packed, the boxes taped and labeled,
and a babysitter played go fish on the porch
with the son and toddler daughter.
The windshield gleamed. A chip, thumbnail-wide,
explained the clouds' share of weakness.
I had an image to protect—
my face hovering, my friend's near it,
frown spidering glimpse, how I'd remember this,
and the rest. That's all there usually is, these days,
to loss—no violence. We must've dared it
once too often, when absence loomed
its soapstone shadow, tantamount to everything.
Recall, years hence, the shameless scream,
which did not go unpunished, on a day
too much like this. Now we know better. We speak
outside of silence, as we've studied, to forget,
and in between syllables that count out mostly nothing
someone makes the closing gestures—
seat belts tight, dog in carrier.
The exhaust pipe huffs out a sour, sad stench,
and they heave off slow under crush
of essentials, crawling like the future down the wet lane,
tending on dull rubber, the straightaway
far away, and if I am more or less neglected—checking
my pockets idly for despair, or lint—I believe they'll return
to me, settling somewhere. *We'll be in touch,*
we've said aloud, embraced, touched
hands, and the weariness, the bleach-burned sky,
and the calendar, squares carved in lockstep rows,
extend the signal to begin again.

# Petition for a Plastic Procedure

*This is a very unusual list of accomplishments.*
The pencil streaking alongside the pad.
The compass needle abrading north.
*I am not the appropriate judge for this kind of thing.*
You will travel to interview the treasurer.
You will observe and record the sinuous
hallways tiled in a salamander freckle
popular in decades when funds condensed
on cold stone dedicated to commerce
emerged wet-winged and black-lipped.
The first murder victim sprawled
naked in the tall grass of the unoccupied
zone inspired a fresh set of limitations
among visitors, local day trippers
who wanted to view the luggage area.
*Anyone who remembers it was a child then.*
But documented here is a heroism
that suffers no alteration. As morning dives
onto the grenade of afternoon, evening's
damp retreats, siphoned into the air,
invisibly, in a performance of the kind
of elementary scientific theory everyone
forgets. *I will save you.* Early to rise,
early to services, the plume in the hat,
and a quick, furtive adjustment, snap.
The chin lists like a ship. A white woman
in a white house. To exit—French doors,
carpets, the provocative bloom of a beam
of sunlight creeping to the threshold
of an urgent need for shade—how smooth
the lapping of first into second, opposite
to opposed. And isn't to expect magnetism
—the closeness of brothers, for starters,
who parse the rapid tread of the fox,

the floating above twig and brush
that silently bespeaks reward—
exactly what shoves you like a gust
at the window? Wait your turn. How desire
hummed at the aperture—couldn't the first
person speak firstly, just this once?
*This is a very tall order of groceries.* The broken
stub of lead clutching a knotted string.
The gray stain. The calendar, the squares,
breakfast cereal. *When might you be available?*
*Would you care for a bottle of liniment?*
*How scrawl the lineaments of your intentions?*
Geographically speaking, this is the middle
of the end. You cough and it tastes funny.
You butcher a joke and it goes on your c.v.
*You probably shouldn't bring that up again.*
In this context the idea of the "cerebral"
seems almost insulting. Shouldn't you
be getting undressed? The silken frogs
chirping in your blouse. The fingernails,
the poor diet, the neurosis of posture,
the tsk tsk, someone has to be on top.
*Every time I went through a break-up*
*somebody got his tires slashed.*
*But I was too savvy to allow photographs.*
Savor it, darling, savor it. Clover honey,
milk, the best bar on St. Patrick's day.
Now spring ushers in the jackbird's hammer.
The bark matches the leaves, the tongue
negotiates the difficulties, the new words
dance the can-can and the can't-can't,
the lord of disappearings leaps out
of the dark woods, and there's almost a tussle
in the background. Apparently the experts
know what's inside your eyes besides gelatin.
*And how long did you live in the city before*

*you developed a longing for simpler music?*
You don't want to master the break of bad news.
But it's your fault. Anybody with class
would've fought you and did but they lost.
The green glass reflects the opacity of the brow.
The glass candlesticks collect dust where
in the days of wine and murder pomegranate
wax melted. A short man and a rich man
walked into a bar and a kangaroo searched
its pouch for money to pay them.
Nothing had changed and it wasn't going to.
Some people like to talk about choices.
If you walk to your closet and the door
will not budge. If the icy wind races
your breath to the river. One poor girl
can spoil the whole barrel. *I meant it
like that*, she says. And the room,
apologetically restrained, decides to melt
into the arms of happy accident.

# Quadriptych

I.

We called it our lair of picnic blankets and old mistakes.
I'd watch you dig down under styrofoam for the comic books
and highlighter pens: we knew how to have fun, and drawing
had something to do with all our afternoons fearing the worst.
The magazines said the American trend of t-shirts with words
had caught on, and they didn't have to make sense as long
as the cotton was pink and gold. Mom told us about middy
blouses and the World Wars: our shero, when she caught us
playing cards without rules and we wrapped our arms
around her knees and she drove us later to the mechanic's shop.


II.

"Nowadays when somebody gets killed you can't tell
if the mourners wanted to clean out their garage or what,"
he says, inscribing the day's lesson under his sleepy eyes
with black Sharpie. "That'll never come off," she replies,
if you can call it a reply when someone changes the subject
to the apropos, like the flag, or the 1980s, the fashions
we're embarrassed to admit we miss, still a bargain
in some chic corners of the globe, like socks or cloches
or rubber watches. Once I received a packet of yarn
all the way from Italy, and I hadn't even ordered or paid.

III.

I snipped the corners of the envelope and my cuticles bled,
but I'd been chewing them, prying loose divots of skin
that tasted like black pepper. I always try to do things right.
For today's performance, classic games or that episode
of *Columbo* in which an ambitious chess player with attitude
murders his rival? Or we could bust into Mommy's make-up
and paint our body parts, or spray the backyard bees with gold leaf
except then we'd really be in trouble. So much nostalgia,
so little time: I loved you more when you were vivid
and vibrated and your open mouth breathed the sweetest.


IV.

O perfection of past glories, now more alive than in their day
of cellophane and crayon, when are you coming for me,
really? Have you only been teasing, dangling your sloppy
hose? I have come to doubt this balance, like a plate of beans
on the knees at the church picnic—and the blanket! We spread
its unfolded segments out like puzzle pieces. We overlapped.
I hadn't yet picked up my habit of wearing a visor but someday
I would lose an eye. The crown marked STILL FIVE CENTS,
and our trust in those promises—now we know how right
we were, and now we fight for the rich man's ticket.

# Locked Fault

More than 230 earthquakes with a magnitude greater than
3.0 have shaken the state of Oklahoma already this year.
Before 2008 the state averaged one such quake a year.
—*Scientific American*, July 3, 2014

We never expected the quivering
The leaves tried to hide. Tendrils curled
Inward like fingers blaming the stem.
Then the cautious click the window frame slipped
Like a teacher at the podium clearing her throat
To begin, again, the maps to memorize.
In this country all roads crossed to remind us
To kneel beneath something solid enough
To break a blow. We trudged the neighborhood
Recording road cracks. We measured
The upshot of grass. As modern people
We spooled our, asking *what*
Till the light answered *yes* and *we felt it*
And *right underneath, I almost looked.*
Solid space propped our house above
Piers and concrete. Old metal
Sheared us up and together, oak to stone,
Brick to bolt and back. We tied down fire.
We nailed up straps. Outside no one picketed
Like the crowds in the cities we read about.
No one wrote letters or laws. Some mornings
We woke to thunder and downpour
Like a mob demanding passage through
Mountain walls, but this was flatland
And the cries we heard were drops
And gushing. We dreamed we swam
To another country, where rigs never rose
Above the modesty of fields and the legs

Of the horses were free of sores and we could keep
Quiet on our porches at night. But any minute
The cornerstones might pierce their own hearts
With iron rods. When the trucks unloaded
Their needles, the vast hammers to pound
Deep as blood, we lived up to what we'd been taught
About gods and rocks and the way to handle
Strangers. If wrong is what breaks
The silence like plodding, we could not change,
Though the world changed beneath us, shuddering.
We wondered why our prayers rang like coins
Into grates where trash collects in storm.

# Scoop Up Broken

The temper of mourning turned back.
Its hands drove into its pockets
Where the fingers crumbled like sugar.
No wool to be found. No black dice
Carved of maple. The first curve
Of the road, the burdened radius,
Burned in the distance, but no steam
Signaled impending blindness.
The fenceposts and treetrunks refused
To bend. If loss could be counted,
It would hold up its fists, the blunted
Measure worn down. But nothing
Moved. Mourning's own volition
Strained to make out the strand
And the locust grove. What was left
Of the sky boiled like scorched soup.
Anyone could see what had happened,
Upside down, so the falling swept high
And the rising collapsed over its knees
And hugged its own body fattened
On barley before famine and forgetting.
In a painting a boy would be skating.
In a song a woman would tend hens.
Once there was a desert and a man
Who could not get home. He bought
A ticket without a bus. He trained
His legs to kick harder but no rain
Filled the river past the rocks.
The jaws of the great fish grew
Together in swirled stone. Mourning
Could decide whether to stand still
Or to keep walking, but this compass
Pivoted like a sunflower, and the hills

Twinned every direction, now
Multiplying in mosaic like glass
To sand and pebbles. Do not move,
Mourning. Stay close. It's late
And the bottles are full of untested
Poison. You will finish your story
When you remember to wake up
Without remembering. But even then
A clock strike or a bamboo rug
Could weave across your future
Like a wall there is no climbing,
Only keeping, like an old saucer,
A card taped to the bottom with a date
And a message intended to be read
Only upon the occasion of fracture
And sweeping, sweeping of shards.

# Cormorant

*summer 2010*

I shine the point of this pencil
        across the spangle
of a single word.
        Old, disgraced nouns—
what to call anyone?

If you're smart, you'll go
        out of your way.
She doesn't have to
        help you.
*It's Eclipse day*, she says.

*My daughter bought tickets.*
        She's squaring the space
behind a desk.
        She's an "administrative assistant,"
impudent as cracked glass,

slapping down the stupid Ph.D.'s,
        trapped in their freedoms,
bothering sheets of paper.
        They cross the office floor like ducks.
Because I've met the daughter

I imagine her in flip-flops,
        shyness, pink rhinestone,
shuffling forward heel to toe,
        desperate
queue, more girls than boys.

She doesn't listen for
        certain words
outside a theater,
        here in Oklahoma
where women kneel

to cold-blooded floors—
        low-budget gods—
backs of hands knotted like birch roots—
        never having been anywhere
beyond rooms

where Fox or CNN chatters
        like a clutch of ordinary sparrows
nestbound, fledgling,
        beaks gaped, to be jabbed into by a parent,
the violence same as everything,

forced into life,
        then death.
There exist shimmering screens
        like oceans.
There exist latter-day journalists,

absence, drill strings,
        authorities, arrest.
There exist landscapes,
        fixation,
stopped like no machine emergency,

handcuffed, unpardoned—
        not in that sense. No sense.
Like any curious intruder who strolls,
        or did, once,
    beaches more or less unwatched,

unsurveilled,
        one pier to another,
those lonely arms of enterprise
        small in their way, in the way.
I too dread the story's moral,

the vampire vomiting its cloak of oil, all 27,000
        vampires I hadn't known how to count
until some disappointed prophet
        recited the statistics;
and like any other sexy vampire

offering the modest women
        of Oklahoma something to wait up for
it bathes in night light.
        I reload the video feed,
a gush swaying like a cobra.

And though this year
        is the year of vampires
and clotless bleeding
        and the sexuality—the sex,
sexing—of the dead

and women admitting they are eels
        of yearning who never get enough
drilling that only occasionally
        explodes and forges
dark vaults and fires combustion

engines all the way to Planet XXX,
        scholars hunker
into swank laptops
        and declare all this a positive sign,
vampires stand for The Other

and we love them because now we love
        The Other;
and there are funerals to attend,
        friends painted inside like ghosts,
many-fingered swaths of white matter.

I am observing these several dramas.
        I am often unable to comment,
as if chewing an ice cube,
        tongue fat as a hammer,
and the black-hatted

vamp droops his face to my quivering
        and asks if I need
a ride, we gas up at the pump, fine leather
        a pillow for my virginity, and I'm changed,
one-two.

But I won't go.
        These last hours furious, shrieking
as in the aria of a mythic bird—
        a cormorant—that has lost its mate,
it's the last specimen

in creation, and it's looking to hurt
        somebody, it doesn't want
documentation, it doesn't want to stuff its babies
        on bottle caps,
the profiles jigsawing the horizon,

it might not be a scholar
        but it knows when the seas it fished
stink like a strip of celluloid
        women in Oklahoma weep to
because it reminds them of their lives,

and what else could they want but to fling
        breast-first into sludge?
The bird is burdened with the sense
        it knows everything.
It soars like a magnet over waves

that curl, flatten,
        spell, reverberate, and here on my desk
where nobody is allowed
        scrolls of sorry untruths are as dead
as tomes of forgettable glories

and the secretaries
      win Admin. Assistant of the Year Award bouquets,
nightly yielding
      beneath someone who pays the bills,
always the geometry of the cell,

rhomboid of the veneered desk,
      and the cell phone
and the aberrant cell
      that splits its way triumphant
into a tumor gouging out silent

and the fury of sea creatures
      in a year or two hatched eyeless
and photographs and petitions—
      taxpayers and debts—
delusions of omniscience—

inability to wake up alert—
      harassers and shooters and sun
braiding the blinds and the wingspan—
      the feathers; the choking
on bones; the flight—

and the world is
      somehow the same down there—
light gathering across gleaming waters—
      but the world, oh
glory, oh scheme and sheen, is not the same.

# About the Author

Lisa Lewis's previous books include *The Unbeliever* (Brittingham Prize), *Silent Treatment* (National Poetry Series), *Vivisect* (New Issues Press), *Burned House with Swimming Pool* (*American Poetry Journal* Prize, Dream Horse Press), and *The Body Double* (*Georgetown Review* Press). A chapbook titled *Story Box* was also published as winner of the Poetry West Chapbook Contest.

Her work has appeared in numerous literary magazines and anthologies, including *Kenyon Review, New England Review, Washington Square, Third Coast, American Literary Review, Fence, Seattle Review,* and *Best American Poetry.* She has also won awards from the *American Poetry Review* and the *Missouri Review,* a Pushcart Prize and an NEA Fellowship. She teaches in the creative writing program at Oklahoma State University, which she directed from 1999 through 2016, and serves as poetry editor for the *Cimarron Review.*

# About the Artist

Brenda Goodman is an artist and painter currently living and working in Pine Hill, New York. Her artistic practice includes paintings, works on paper, and sculptures. Her work has been exhibited at numerous galleries and museums, including recent one-person exhibitions at Jeff Bailey Gallery, the College for Creative Studies Center Galleries, Paul Kotula Projects, and Life on Mars Gallery. Her work has been included in group exhibitions at museums including the Whitney Museum of American Art and the Museum of Contemporary Art in Chicago. Her work has been collected by the Birmingham Museum of Art, the Carnegie Museum of Art, the California Center for the Arts Museum, The John D. and Catherine T. MacArthur Foundation, and many others. Goodman has been a visiting artist at colleges and universities across the United States and Canada including the University of the Arts, the Parsons School of Design, and Bard College.

# About The Word Works

The Word Works, a nonprofit literary organization, publishes contemporary poetry and presents public programs. Other imprints include the Washington Prize, International Editions, and the Hilary Tham Capital Collection. A reading period is also held in May.

Monthly, The Word Works offers free literary programs in the Chevy Chase, MD, Café Muse series, and each summer, it holds free poetry programs in Washington, D.C.'s Rock Creek Park. Annually in June, two high school students debut in the Joaquin Miller Poetry Series as winners of the Jacklyn Potter Young Poets Competition. Since 1974, Word Works programs have included: "In the Shadow of the Capitol," a symposium and archival project on the African American intellectual community in segregated Washington, D.C.; the Gunston Arts Center Poetry Series; the Poet Editor panel discussions at The Writer's Center; and Master Class workshops.

As a 501(c)3 organization, The Word Works has received awards from the National Endowment for the Arts, the National Endowment for the Humanities, the D.C. Commission on the Arts & Humanities, the Witter Bynner Foundation, Poets & Writers, The Writer's Center, Bell Atlantic, the David G. Taft Foundation, and others, including many generous private patrons.

The Word Works has established an archive of artistic and administrative materials in the Washington Writing Archive housed in the George Washington University Gelman Library. It is a member of the Council of Literary Magazines and Presses and its books are distributed by Small Press Distribution.

**wordworksbooks.org**

THE TENTH GATE PRIZE

Jennifer Barber, *Works on Paper*, 2015
Lisa Lewis, *Taxonomy of the Missing*, 2017
Roger Sedarat, *Haji As Puppet*, 2016
Lisa Sewell, *Impossible Object*, 2014

THE WASHINGTON PRIZE

Nathalie F. Anderson, *Following Fred Astaire*, 1998
Michael Atkinson, *One Hundred Children Waiting for a Train*, 2001
Molly Bashaw, *The Whole Field Still Moving Inside It*, 2013
Carrie Bennett, *biography of water*, 2004
Peter Blair, *Last Heat*, 1999
John Bradley, *Love-in-Idleness: The Poetry of Roberto Zingarello*,
    1995, 2ND edition 2014
Christopher Bursk, *The Way Water Rubs Stone*, 1988
Richard Carr, *Ace*, 2008
Jamison Crabtree, *Rel[AM]ent*, 2014
Jessica Cuello, *Hunt*, 2016
Barbara Duffey, *Simple Machines*, 2015
B. K. Fischer, *St. Rage's Vault*, 2012
Linda Lee Harper, *Toward Desire*, 1995
Ann Rae Jonas, *A Diamond Is Hard But Not Tough*, 1997
Susan Lewis, *Zoom*, 2017
Frannie Lindsay, *Mayweed*, 2009
Richard Lyons, *Fleur Carnivore*, 2005
Elaine Magarrell, *Blameless Lives*, 1991
Fred Marchant, *Tipping Point*, 1993, 2ND edition 2013
Ron Mohring, *Survivable World*, 2003
Barbara Moore, *Farewell to the Body*, 1990
Brad Richard, *Motion Studies*, 2010
Jay Rogoff, *The Cutoff*, 1994
Prartho Sereno, *Call from Paris*, 2007, 2ND edition 2013
Enid Shomer, *Stalking the Florida Panther*, 1987
John Surowiecki, *The Hat City After Men Stopped Wearing Hats*, 2006
Miles Waggener, *Phoenix Suites*, 2002
Charlotte Warren, *Gandhi's Lap*, 2000
Mike White, *How to Make a Bird with Two Hands*, 2011
Nancy White, *Sun, Moon, Salt*, 1992, 2ND edition 2010
George Young, *Spinoza's Mouse*, 1996

THE HILARY THAM CAPITAL COLLECTION
Nathalie Anderson, *Stain*
Mel Belin, *Flesh That Was Chrysalis*
Carrie Bennett, *The Land Is a Painted Thing*
Doris Brody, *Judging the Distance*
Sarah Browning, *Whiskey in the Garden of Eden*
Grace Cavalieri, *Pinecrest Rest Haven*
Cheryl Clarke, *By My Precise Haircut*
Christopher Conlon, *Gilbert and Garbo in Love*
        & *Mary Falls: Requiem for Mrs. Surratt*
Donna Denizé, *Broken Like Job*
W. Perry Epes, *Nothing Happened*
David Eye, *Seed*
Bernadette Geyer, *The Scabbard of Her Throat*
Barbara G. S. Hagerty, *Twinzilla*
James Hopkins, *Eight Pale Women*
Donald Illich, *Chance Bodies*
Brandon Johnson, *Love's Skin*
Thomas March, *Aftermath*
Marilyn McCabe, *Perpetual Motion*
Judith McCombs, *The Habit of Fire*
James McEwen, *Snake Country*
Miles David Moore, *The Bears of Paris*
        & *Rollercoaster*
Kathi Morrison-Taylor, *By the Nest*
Tera Vale Ragan, *Reading the Ground*
Michael Shaffner, *The Good Opinion of Squirrels*
Maria Terrone, *The Bodies We Were Loaned*
Hilary Tham, *Bad Names for Women*
        & *Counting*
Barbara Ungar, *Charlotte Brontë, You Ruined My Life*
        & *Immortal Medusa*
Jonathan Vaile, *Blue Cowboy*
Rosemary Winslow, *Green Bodies*
Michele Wolf, *Immersion*
Joe Zealberg, *Covale*

INTERNATIONAL EDITIONS

Kajal Ahmad (Alana Marie Levinson-LaBrosse, Mewan Nahro Said Sofi and Darya Abdul-Karim Ali Najin, trans., with Barbara Goldberg), *Handful of Salt*

Keyne Cheshire (trans.), *Murder at Jagged Rock: A Tragedy by Sophocles*

Jeannette L. Clariond (Curtis Bauer, trans.), *Image of Absence*

Jean Cocteau (Mary-Sherman Willis, trans.), *Grace Notes*

Yoko Danno & James C. Hopkins, *The Blue Door*

Moshe Dor, Barbara Goldberg, Giora Leshem, eds., *The Stones Remember: Native Israeli Poets*

Moshe Dor (Barbara Goldberg, trans.), *Scorched by the Sun*

Lee Sang (Myong-Hee Kim, trans.), *Crow's Eye View: The Infamy of Lee Sang, Korean Poet*

Vladimir Levchev (Henry Taylor, trans.), *Black Book of the Endangered Species*

OTHER WORD WORKS BOOKS

Annik Adey-Babinski, *Okay Cool No Smoking Love Pony*

Karren L. Alenier, *Wandering on the Outside*

Karren L. Alenier, ed., *Whose Woods These Are*

Karren L. Alenier & Miles David Moore, eds., *Winners: A Retrospective of the Washington Prize*

Christopher Bursk, ed., *Cool Fire*

Willa Carroll, *Nerve Chorus*

Grace Cavalieri, *Creature Comforts*

Barbara Goldberg, *Berta Broadfoot and Pepin the Short*

Akua Lezli Hope, *Them Gone*

Frannie Lindsay, *If Mercy*

Elaine Maggarrell, *The Madness of Chefs*

Marilyn McCabe, *Glass Factory*

JoAnne McFarland, *Identifying the Body*

Kevin McLellan, *Ornitheology*

Leslie McGrath, *Feminists Are Passing from Our Lives*

Ann Pelletier, *Letter That Never*

Ayaz Pirani, *Happy You Are Here*

W.T. Pfefferle, *My Coolest Shirt*

Jacklyn Potter, Dwaine Rieves, Gary Stein, eds., *Cabin Fever: Poets at Joaquin Miller's Cabin*

Robert Sargent, *Aspects of a Southern Story*
& *A Woman from Memphis*
Miles Waggener, *Superstition Freeway*
Fritz Ward, *Tsunami Diorama*
Amber West, *Hen & God*
Nancy White, ed., *Word for Word*